This Gratitude Journal

Belongs To:

My life Achievements

1. ....
2. ....
3. ....
4. ....
5. ....
6. ....
7. ....
8. ....
9. ....
10. ....

• •

Things I'm Grateful for

1. ....
2. ....
3. ....
4. ....
5. ....
6. ....
7. ....
8. ....
9. ....
10. ....

People I Appreciate

1. ....
2. ....
3. ....
4. ....
5. ....
6. ....
7. ....
8. ....
9. ....
10. ....

• •

My Favourite Quotes

....
....
....
....
....
....
....
....
....

Today's 5 things
I'm Grateful for

...1.1.4.12021

1. Shelley's friendship.
2. Barb + Sg
3. clear driveway
4. titanium trim + possibility of cutting hair
5. sleep that makes me feel better

1. Cleaned the hot chocolate from office
2. Barb has an appt to Amanda on Wed
3. I felt good yesterday
4.
5.

Today's 5 things
I'm Grateful for

...1.15.12021

Today's 5 things
I'm Grateful for

...1.16.12021

1. Zoom S.Co tonight
2. no weightgain over Christmas
3. 1 day of exercise
4.
5.

1. Certification of J. Biden as next pres.
2. Joyce's change of heart
3. Barb's commitment to balanced diet
4. That I made salmon patties yesterday
    despite low initiative
5.

Today's 5 things
I'm Grateful for

...1.7.1202?

Today's 5 things
I'm Grateful for

...1.18.12021

1. 2cd day of exercise
2. Shelley's phone calls
3. The good that will come from
   the current political upheaval.
4.
5.

Today's 5 things
I'm Grateful for

...1.1.9.1.2021

1. 3 day of exercise
2. accomplished a little on hall tree despite low energy
3. sunroom and fireplace
4.
5.

1. 4 day of exercise
2. lawmakers who adhere to the constitution
3. able to register for vaccine appt
4. realizing class B type camper would allow me to visit sister or attend funeral
5.

Today's 5 things
I'm Grateful for

...1.10.1.2021

• •

My Weekly Notes

This has been a turbulent week in our nation. Wednesday Trumps supporters stormed/vandalized the Capitol building in order to try to keep Trump in office. Covid deaths were over 4000 a day. On the positive side, Governor Whitmer opened up the vaccine to people over 65 and teachers. On a personal note, I have a Nephrology appt scheduled for Feb and need to get blood work done shortly after the 20th. I am not yet sure whether Spanow and MSU are in the Humana network. Many uncertainties in the future days. Just trust + pray. grateful

Today's 5 things
I'm Grateful for

..1.1.11.12021

1. online church
2. news - to know what's happening despite my isolation + solitude
3. remembering to put out the trash
4.
5.

---

1. My doctor participates with Humana
2. ~~I~~ feel better today
3. I got things done yesterday despite sluggishness
4. Shelley's long conversation with Mike
5.

Today's 5 things
I'm Grateful for

..1.12.2021

Today's 5 things
I'm Grateful for

..1.13.2021

1. that I got my right eye done before pandemic
2. Jean's openness to learn my more ~ news
3. that I made upright cuts on tree without incident
4. sun in the sun room
5. $600 I can donate

---

1. afternoon naps when I am feeling sluggish
2. Shelley's call that always seem to pick me up
3. Barb's appt for vaccine
4. Alice's enjoyment of her granddaughter

Today's 5 things
I'm Grateful for

..1.14.2021

5.

Today's 5 things
I'm Grateful for

......1.....1......

1.
2.
3.
4.
5.

Today's 5 things
I'm Grateful for

...1.1.16.1.2021

1. for a new day, fresh start
2.
3.
4.
5.

1.
2.
3.
4.
5.

Today's 5 things
I'm Grateful for

......1....1......

My Weekly Notes

Well, I got in a slump the end of this week.
The Sunday morning news led me to the
realization that things might not ever get
back to normal at least for me. It will
all depend on how long immunity lasts
and how the virus mutates. So it no longer
seemed reasonable to think of doing a van
conversion and driving to see my sisters in
the fall (just when my immunity might be
waning.) So, it is one day at a time & God.

Today's 5 things
I'm Grateful for

....../....../......

1. ....
2. ....
3. ....
4. ....
5. ....

1. Barb to stimulate me c̄ a new book
2. learning how badly sugar makes me feel
3. ....
4. ....
5. ....

Today's 5 things
I'm Grateful for

.../..19../2021

Today's 5 things
I'm Grateful for

.../..20./2021

1. a vaccine appt on The 28th
2. my snow guy
3. It is inaugration day !!!
4. I ate a little better yesterday
5. Barb got me an interesting book to read

1. new president (Biden/Harris)
2. small group
3. morning sun in sunroom
4. ....
5. ....

Today's 5 things
I'm Grateful for

.../..21./2021

Today's 5 things
I'm Grateful for

.../..22./2021

1. a gray day c̄ light snow
2. getting blood work done at Frandor
3. that my hair trimmer was shipped
4. my blood work was essentially normal
5. ....

Today's 5 things I'm Grateful for

...1...23.12021

1. sunshine in the morning
2. Joe Biden + Gretchen Whitmer
3. The years I could spent a Alice
4. Small dietary changes that make me feel better.
5.

1.
2.
3.
4.
5.

Today's 5 things I'm Grateful for

......./...../......

My Weekly Notes

So the Trump presidency has finally ended and we begin anew with Pres Biden. There is much change to hope for and likely many changes I am not really eager to accept. It seems I will need to learn a whole new set of guidelines for navigating life in the post-Covid years. I am still considering doing a van conversion so I can travel to my sisters (visit or funeral) but it seems a bit daunting to travel alone. Only God knows the future.

Today's 5 things
I'm Grateful for

..1...125.12021

1. Went to church yesterday via video
2. a good night of sleep
3. ....
4. ....
5. ....

1. ....
2. ....
3. ....
4. ....
5. ....

Today's 5 things
I'm Grateful for

......1....1......

Today's 5 things
I'm Grateful for

...1..127.12021

1. snow guy + finding cleek
2. a good night's sleep
3. pickup groceries
4. all the people working to vaccinate us
5. ....

1. small group.
2. visit c Barb
3. petting Billy the cat
4. ....
5. ....

Today's 5 things
I'm Grateful for

...1..128.12021

Today's 5 things
I'm Grateful for

..1..129.12021

1. got my 1st Covid vaccine
2. MSU BB despite how they played
3. how Barb stimulates me with books
4. Shelley's calls
5. easy grocery pickup
   arrival of titanium trim

Today's 5 things
I'm Grateful for
...1.130.12021

1. sunshine, esp in am → sun room
2. warm shelter
3. abundance of food
4. ....
5. ....

1. ....
2. ....
3. ....
4. ....
5. ....

Today's 5 things
I'm Grateful for
......./...../......

My Weekly Notes

This was a good week. Got my 1st Covid vaccine and scheduled the 2nd for Feb 18. Got to see Barb in person for a few minutes. Had several good nights of sleep -- seems to be able to lay on my back more. Scheduled dental appts for March. Nationwide Covid cases are still high but hospitalizations are down -- a couple of days ē 4000 death. Michigan is doing well with ~ 2000 cases a day, down from 8-10,000 a day ~ 1st of Dec. Finally got some snow but I didn't fall on days I needed to go out.

Grateful

Today's 5 things
I'm Grateful for

..21.1..12021

1. televisim to keep me in touch
2. Salmon patties - taste great + healthy
3.
4.
5.

1. morning sun
2. that my Covid vaccine rx only lasted a few hours
3. an old movie to watch while feeling yucky
4.
5.

Today's 5 things
I'm Grateful for

..2.12..12021

Today's 5 things
I'm Grateful for

..2.13..12021

1. good b.p. at Drs appt.
2. easy in & out at Drs appt.
3. MSU BB despite another loss
4. sun in the morning
5.

1. sun in The morning
2. S.G. for some connection to others
3. no longer have hair in my eyes
4.
5.

Today's 5 things
I'm Grateful for

..2.14..12021

Today's 5 things
I'm Grateful for

..2.15..12021

1. long chat c Jean, she is well
2. beauty of fresh snow
3. my snow guy
4. a great day to get gas & mail
5.

Today's 5 things
I'm Grateful for

..... / ..... / .....

1. ....
2. ....
3. ....
4. ....
5. ....

1. ....
2. ....
3. ....
4. ....
5. ....

Today's 5 things
I'm Grateful for

..... / ..... / .....

• •

My Weekly Notes

....
....
....
....
....
....
....
....
....
....

Today's 5 things
I'm Grateful for

...../...../......

1. ....
2. ....
3. ....
4. ....
5. ....

1. ....
2. ....
3. ....
4. ....
5. ....

Today's 5 things
I'm Grateful for

...../...../......

Today's 5 things
I'm Grateful for

...../...../......

1. ....
2. ....
3. ....
4. ....
5. ....

1. ....
2. ....
3. ....
4. ....
5. ....

Today's 5 things
I'm Grateful for

...../...../......

Today's 5 things
I'm Grateful for

...../...../......

1. ....
2. ....
3. ....
4. ....
5. ....

Today's 5 things
I'm Grateful for

....../....../......

1. ....
2. ....
3. ....
4. ....
5. ....

1. ....
2. ....
3. ....
4. ....
5. ....

Today's 5 things
I'm Grateful for

....../....../......

• •

My Weekly Notes

....
....
....
....
....
....
....
....
....
....

Today's 5 things
I'm Grateful for

...../...../.....

1. ....
2. ....
3. ....
4. ....
5. ....

1. ....
2. ....
3. ....
4. ....
5. ....

Today's 5 things
I'm Grateful for

...../...../.....

Today's 5 things
I'm Grateful for

...../...../.....

1. ....
2. ....
3. ....
4. ....
5. ....

1. ....
2. ....
3. ....
4. ....
5. ....

Today's 5 things
I'm Grateful for

...../...../.....

Today's 5 things
I'm Grateful for

...../...../.....

1. ....
2. ....
3. ....
4. ....
5. ....

Today's 5 things
I'm Grateful for

......./....../......

1. ....
2. ....
3. ....
4. ....
5. ....

1. ....
2. ....
3. ....
4. ....
5. ....

Today's 5 things
I'm Grateful for

......./....../......

• •

My Weekly Notes

....
....
....
....
....
....
....
....
....
....

Today's 5 things
I'm Grateful for

.....*/*.....*/*.....

1. ....
2. ....
3. ....
4. ....
5. ....

1. ....
2. ....
3. ....
4. ....
5. ....

Today's 5 things
I'm Grateful for

.....*/*.....*/*.....

Today's 5 things
I'm Grateful for

.....*/*.....*/*.....

1. ....
2. ....
3. ....
4. ....
5. ....

1. ....
2. ....
3. ....
4. ....
5. ....

Today's 5 things
I'm Grateful for

.....*/*.....*/*.....

Today's 5 things
I'm Grateful for

.....*/*.....*/*.....

1. ....
2. ....
3. ....
4. ....
5. ....

Today's 5 things
I'm Grateful for

....../....../......

1. ....
2. ....
3. ....
4. ....
5. ....

1. ....
2. ....
3. ....
4. ....
5. ....

Today's 5 things
I'm Grateful for

....../....../......

• •

My Weekly Notes

....
....
....
....
....
....
....
....
....
....

Today's 5 things
I'm Grateful for

...../...../......

1...
2...
3...
4...
5...

1...
2...
3...
4...
5...

Today's 5 things
I'm Grateful for

...../...../......

Today's 5 things
I'm Grateful for

...../...../......

1...
2...
3...
4...
5...

1...
2...
3...
4...
5...

Today's 5 things
I'm Grateful for

...../...../......

Today's 5 things
I'm Grateful for

...../...../......

1...
2...
3...
4...
5...

Today's 5 things
I'm Grateful for

......./....../......

1. ....
2. ....
3. ....
4. ....
5. ....

1. ....
2. ....
3. ....
4. ....
5. ....

Today's 5 things
I'm Grateful for

......./....../......

• •

My Weekly Notes

....
....
....
....
....
....
....
....
....
....

Today's 5 things
I'm Grateful for

...../...../.....

1. ....
2. ....
3. ....
4. ....
5. ....

1. ....
2. ....
3. ....
4. ....
5. ....

Today's 5 things
I'm Grateful for

...../...../.....

Today's 5 things
I'm Grateful for

...../...../.....

1. ....
2. ....
3. ....
4. ....
5. ....

1. ....
2. ....
3. ....
4. ....
5. ....

Today's 5 things
I'm Grateful for

...../...../.....

Today's 5 things
I'm Grateful for

...../...../.....

1. ....
2. ....
3. ....
4. ....
5. ....

Today's 5 things
I'm Grateful for

......./....../......

1. ....
2. ....
3. ....
4. ....
5. ....

1. ....
2. ....
3. ....
4. ....
5. ....

Today's 5 things
I'm Grateful for

......./....../......

• •

My Weekly Notes

....
....
....
....
....
....
....
....
....
....

Today's 5 things
I'm Grateful for

...../...../......

1. ....
2. ....
3. ....
4. ....
5. ....

1. ....
2. ....
3. ....
4. ....
5. ....

Today's 5 things
I'm Grateful for

...../...../......

Today's 5 things
I'm Grateful for

...../...../......

1. ....
2. ....
3. ....
4. ....
5. ....

1. ....
2. ....
3. ....
4. ....
5. ....

Today's 5 things
I'm Grateful for

...../...../......

Today's 5 things
I'm Grateful for

...../...../......

1. ....
2. ....
3. ....
4. ....
5. ....

Today's 5 things
I'm Grateful for

......./....../......

1. ....
2. ....
3. ....
4. ....
5. ....

1. ....
2. ....
3. ....
4. ....
5. ....

Today's 5 things
I'm Grateful for

......./....../......

• •

My Weekly Notes

....
....
....
....
....
....
....
....
....
....

Today's 5 things
I'm Grateful for

...../...../......

1. ....
2. ....
3. ....
4. ....
5. ....

1. ....
2. ....
3. ....
4. ....
5. ....

Today's 5 things
I'm Grateful for

...../...../......

Today's 5 things
I'm Grateful for

...../...../......

1. ....
2. ....
3. ....
4. ....
5. ....

1. ....
2. ....
3. ....
4. ....
5. ....

Today's 5 things
I'm Grateful for

...../...../......

Today's 5 things
I'm Grateful for

...../...../......

1. ....
2. ....
3. ....
4. ....
5. ....

Today's 5 things
I'm Grateful for

......./...../......

1. ....
2. ....
3. ....
4. ....
5. ....

1. ....
2. ....
3. ....
4. ....
5. ....

Today's 5 things
I'm Grateful for

......./...../......

My Weekly Notes

....
....
....
....
....
....
....
....
....
....

Today's 5 things
I'm Grateful for

......./......./......

1. ....
2. ....
3. ....
4. ....
5. ....

1. ....
2. ....
3. ....
4. ....
5. ....

Today's 5 things
I'm Grateful for

......./......./......

Today's 5 things
I'm Grateful for

......./......./......

1. ....
2. ....
3. ....
4. ....
5. ....

1. ....
2. ....
3. ....
4. ....
5. ....

Today's 5 things
I'm Grateful for

......./......./......

Today's 5 things
I'm Grateful for

......./......./......

1. ....
2. ....
3. ....
4. ....
5. ....

Today's 5 things
I'm Grateful for

....../...../......

1. ....
2. ....
3. ....
4. ....
5. ....

1. ....
2. ....
3. ....
4. ....
5. ....

Today's 5 things
I'm Grateful for

....../...../......

My Weekly Notes

....
....
....
....
....
....
....
....
....
....

Today's 5 things
I'm Grateful for

....../...../......

1. ....
2. ....
3. ....
4. ....
5. ....

1. ....
2. ....
3. ....
4. ....
5. ....

Today's 5 things
I'm Grateful for

....../...../......

Today's 5 things
I'm Grateful for

....../...../......

1. ....
2. ....
3. ....
4. ....
5. ....

1. ....
2. ....
3. ....
4. ....
5. ....

Today's 5 things
I'm Grateful for

....../...../......

Today's 5 things
I'm Grateful for

....../...../......

1. ....
2. ....
3. ....
4. ....
5. ....

Today's 5 things
I'm Grateful for

....../...../......

1. ....
2. ....
3. ....
4. ....
5. ....

1. ....
2. ....
3. ....
4. ....
5. ....

Today's 5 things
I'm Grateful for

....../...../......

• •

My Weekly Notes

....
....
....
....
....
....
....
....
....
....

Today's 5 things
I'm Grateful for

...../...../......

1. ....
2. ....
3. ....
4. ....
5. ....

1. ....
2. ....
3. ....
4. ....
5. ....

Today's 5 things
I'm Grateful for

...../...../......

Today's 5 things
I'm Grateful for

...../...../......

1. ....
2. ....
3. ....
4. ....
5. ....

1. ....
2. ....
3. ....
4. ....
5. ....

Today's 5 things
I'm Grateful for

...../...../......

Today's 5 things
I'm Grateful for

...../...../......

1. ....
2. ....
3. ....
4. ....
5. ....

Today's 5 things
I'm Grateful for

...../...../......

1. ....
2. ....
3. ....
4. ....
5. ....

1. ....
2. ....
3. ....
4. ....
5. ....

Today's 5 things
I'm Grateful for

...../...../......

• •

My Weekly Notes

....
....
....
....
....
....
....
....
....

Today's 5 things
I'm Grateful for

......./....../......

1. ....
2. ....
3. ....
4. ....
5. ....

1. ....
2. ....
3. ....
4. ....
5. ....

Today's 5 things
I'm Grateful for

......./....../......

Today's 5 things
I'm Grateful for

......./....../......

1. ....
2. ....
3. ....
4. ....
5. ....

1. ....
2. ....
3. ....
4. ....
5. ....

Today's 5 things
I'm Grateful for

......./....../......

Today's 5 things
I'm Grateful for

......./....../......

1. ....
2. ....
3. ....
4. ....
5. ....

Today's 5 things
I'm Grateful for

......./....../......

1. ....
2. ....
3. ....
4. ....
5. ....

1. ....
2. ....
3. ....
4. ....
5. ....

Today's 5 things
I'm Grateful for

......./....../......

My Weekly Notes

....
....
....
....
....
....
....
....
....

Today's 5 things
I'm Grateful for

......./....../......

1. ....
2. ....
3. ....
4. ....
5. ....

1. ....
2. ....
3. ....
4. ....
5. ....

Today's 5 things
I'm Grateful for

......./....../......

Today's 5 things
I'm Grateful for

......./....../......

1. ....
2. ....
3. ....
4. ....
5. ....

1. ....
2. ....
3. ....
4. ....
5. ....

Today's 5 things
I'm Grateful for

......./....../......

Today's 5 things
I'm Grateful for

......./....../......

1. ....
2. ....
3. ....
4. ....
5. ....

Today's 5 things
I'm Grateful for

...... / ..... / ......

1. ....
2. ....
3. ....
4. ....
5. ....

1. ....
2. ....
3. ....
4. ....
5. ....

Today's 5 things
I'm Grateful for

...... / ..... / ......

• •

My Weekly Notes

....
....
....
....
....
....
....
....
....
....

Today's 5 things
I'm Grateful for

...../...../......

1. ....
2. ....
3. ....
4. ....
5. ....

1. ....
2. ....
3. ....
4. ....
5. ....

Today's 5 things
I'm Grateful for

...../...../......

Today's 5 things
I'm Grateful for

...../...../......

1. ....
2. ....
3. ....
4. ....
5. ....

1. ....
2. ....
3. ....
4. ....
5. ....

Today's 5 things
I'm Grateful for

...../...../......

Today's 5 things
I'm Grateful for

...../...../......

1. ....
2. ....
3. ....
4. ....
5. ....

Today's 5 things
I'm Grateful for

...../...../......

1. ....
2. ....
3. ....
4. ....
5. ....

1. ....
2. ....
3. ....
4. ....
5. ....

Today's 5 things
I'm Grateful for

...../...../......

My Weekly Notes

....
....
....
....
....
....
....
....
....
....

Today's 5 things
I'm Grateful for

...../...../.....

1. ....
2. ....
3. ....
4. ....
5. ....

1. ....
2. ....
3. ....
4. ....
5. ....

Today's 5 things
I'm Grateful for

...../...../.....

Today's 5 things
I'm Grateful for

...../...../.....

1. ....
2. ....
3. ....
4. ....
5. ....

1. ....
2. ....
3. ....
4. ....
5. ....

Today's 5 things
I'm Grateful for

...../...../.....

Today's 5 things
I'm Grateful for

...../...../.....

1. ....
2. ....
3. ....
4. ....
5. ....

Today's 5 things
I'm Grateful for

......./...../......

1. ....
2. ....
3. ....
4. ....
5. ....

1. ....
2. ....
3. ....
4. ....
5. ....

Today's 5 things
I'm Grateful for

......./...../......

• •

My Weekly Notes

....
....
....
....
....
....
....
....
....
....

Today's 5 things
I'm Grateful for

...../...../......

1. ....
2. ....
3. ....
4. ....
5. ....

1. ....
2. ....
3. ....
4. ....
5. ....

Today's 5 things
I'm Grateful for

...../...../......

Today's 5 things
I'm Grateful for

...../...../......

1. ....
2. ....
3. ....
4. ....
5. ....

1. ....
2. ....
3. ....
4. ....
5. ....

Today's 5 things
I'm Grateful for

...../...../......

Today's 5 things
I'm Grateful for

...../...../......

1. ....
2. ....
3. ....
4. ....
5. ....

Today's 5 things
I'm Grateful for

......../....../......

1...
2...
3...
4...
5...

1...
2...
3...
4...
5...

Today's 5 things
I'm Grateful for

......../....../......

• •

My Weekly Notes

....
....
....
....
....
....
....
....
....
....

Today's 5 things
I'm Grateful for

...../...../......

1. ....
2. ....
3. ....
4. ....
5. ....

1. ....
2. ....
3. ....
4. ....
5. ....

Today's 5 things
I'm Grateful for

...../...../......

Today's 5 things
I'm Grateful for

...../...../......

1. ....
2. ....
3. ....
4. ....
5. ....

1. ....
2. ....
3. ....
4. ....
5. ....

Today's 5 things
I'm Grateful for

...../...../......

Today's 5 things
I'm Grateful for

...../...../......

1. ....
2. ....
3. ....
4. ....
5. ....

Today's 5 things
I'm Grateful for

....../...../......

1. ....
2. ....
3. ....
4. ....
5. ....

1. ....
2. ....
3. ....
4. ....
5. ....

Today's 5 things
I'm Grateful for

....../...../......

· ·

My Weekly Notes

....
....
....
....
....
....
....
....
....
....

Today's 5 things
I'm Grateful for

...../..../......

1. ....
2. ....
3. ....
4. ....
5. ....

1. ....
2. ....
3. ....
4. ....
5. ....

Today's 5 things
I'm Grateful for

...../..../......

Today's 5 things
I'm Grateful for

...../..../......

1. ....
2. ....
3. ....
4. ....
5. ....

1. ....
2. ....
3. ....
4. ....
5. ....

Today's 5 things
I'm Grateful for

...../..../......

Today's 5 things
I'm Grateful for

...../..../......

1. ....
2. ....
3. ....
4. ....
5. ....

Today's 5 things
I'm Grateful for

..... / ..... / .....

1. ....
2. ....
3. ....
4. ....
5. ....

1. ....
2. ....
3. ....
4. ....
5. ....

Today's 5 things
I'm Grateful for

..... / ..... / .....

• •

My Weekly Notes

....
....
....
....
....
....
....
....
....

Today's 5 things
I'm Grateful for

...../...../.....

1. ....
2. ....
3. ....
4. ....
5. ....

1. ....
2. ....
3. ....
4. ....
5. ....

Today's 5 things
I'm Grateful for

...../...../.....

Today's 5 things
I'm Grateful for

...../...../.....

1. ....
2. ....
3. ....
4. ....
5. ....

1. ....
2. ....
3. ....
4. ....
5. ....

Today's 5 things
I'm Grateful for

...../...../.....

Today's 5 things
I'm Grateful for

...../...../.....

1. ....
2. ....
3. ....
4. ....
5. ....

Today's 5 things
I'm Grateful for

....../...../......

1. ....
2. ....
3. ....
4. ....
5. ....

1. ....
2. ....
3. ....
4. ....
5. ....

Today's 5 things
I'm Grateful for

....../...../......

· ·

My Weekly Notes

....
....
....
....
....
....
....
....
....
....

Today's 5 things
I'm Grateful for

....../...../......

1. ....
2. ....
3. ....
4. ....
5. ....

1. ....
2. ....
3. ....
4. ....
5. ....

Today's 5 things
I'm Grateful for

....../...../......

Today's 5 things
I'm Grateful for

....../...../......

1. ....
2. ....
3. ....
4. ....
5. ....

1. ....
2. ....
3. ....
4. ....
5. ....

Today's 5 things
I'm Grateful for

....../...../......

Today's 5 things
I'm Grateful for

....../...../......

1. ....
2. ....
3. ....
4. ....
5. ....

Today's 5 things
I'm Grateful for

....../...../......

1. ....
2. ....
3. ....
4. ....
5. ....

1. ....
2. ....
3. ....
4. ....
5. ....

Today's 5 things
I'm Grateful for

....../...../......

• •

My Weekly Notes

....
....
....
....
....
....
....
....
....
....

Today's 5 things
I'm Grateful for

....../...../......

1. ....
2. ....
3. ....
4. ....
5. ....

1. ....
2. ....
3. ....
4. ....
5. ....

Today's 5 things
I'm Grateful for

....../...../......

Today's 5 things
I'm Grateful for

....../...../......

1. ....
2. ....
3. ....
4. ....
5. ....

1. ....
2. ....
3. ....
4. ....
5. ....

Today's 5 things
I'm Grateful for

....../...../......

Today's 5 things
I'm Grateful for

....../...../......

1. ....
2. ....
3. ....
4. ....
5. ....

Today's 5 things
I'm Grateful for

......./....../......

1. ....
2. ....
3. ....
4. ....
5. ....

1. ....
2. ....
3. ....
4. ....
5. ....

Today's 5 things
I'm Grateful for

......./....../......

• •

My Weekly Notes

....
....
....
....
....
....
....
....
....
....

Today's 5 things
I'm Grateful for

...../...../......

1. ....
2. ....
3. ....
4. ....
5. ....

1. ....
2. ....
3. ....
4. ....
5. ....

Today's 5 things
I'm Grateful for

...../...../......

Today's 5 things
I'm Grateful for

...../...../......

1. ....
2. ....
3. ....
4. ....
5. ....

1. ....
2. ....
3. ....
4. ....
5. ....

Today's 5 things
I'm Grateful for

...../...../......

Today's 5 things
I'm Grateful for

...../...../......

1. ....
2. ....
3. ....
4. ....
5. ....

Today's 5 things
I'm Grateful for

...../...../......

1. ....

2. ....

3. ....

4. ....

5. ....

1. ....

2. ....

3. ....

4. ....

5. ....

Today's 5 things
I'm Grateful for

...../...../......

• •

My Weekly Notes

....

....

....

....

....

....

....

....

....

....

Today's 5 things
I'm Grateful for

...../...../......

1. ....
2. ....
3. ....
4. ....
5. ....

1. ....
2. ....
3. ....
4. ....
5. ....

Today's 5 things
I'm Grateful for

...../...../......

Today's 5 things
I'm Grateful for

...../...../......

1. ....
2. ....
3. ....
4. ....
5. ....

1. ....
2. ....
3. ....
4. ....
5. ....

Today's 5 things
I'm Grateful for

...../...../......

Today's 5 things
I'm Grateful for

...../...../......

1. ....
2. ....
3. ....
4. ....
5. ....

Today's 5 things
I'm Grateful for

......./....../......

1. ....
2. ....
3. ....
4. ....
5. ....

1. ....
2. ....
3. ....
4. ....
5. ....

Today's 5 things
I'm Grateful for

......./....../......

• •

My Weekly Notes

....
....
....
....
....
....
....
....
....
....

Today's 5 things
I'm Grateful for

...../...../......

1. ....
2. ....
3. ....
4. ....
5. ....

1. ....
2. ....
3. ....
4. ....
5. ....

Today's 5 things
I'm Grateful for

...../...../......

Today's 5 things
I'm Grateful for

...../...../......

1. ....
2. ....
3. ....
4. ....
5. ....

1. ....
2. ....
3. ....
4. ....
5. ....

Today's 5 things
I'm Grateful for

...../...../......

Today's 5 things
I'm Grateful for

...../...../......

1. ....
2. ....
3. ....
4. ....
5. ....

Today's 5 things
I'm Grateful for

......./...../.....

1. ....
2. ....
3. ....
4. ....
5. ....

1. ....
2. ....
3. ....
4. ....
5. ....

Today's 5 things
I'm Grateful for

......./...../.....

· ·

My Weekly Notes

....
....
....
....
....
....
....
....
....
....

Today's 5 things
I'm Grateful for

......./....../......

1. ....
2. ....
3. ....
4. ....
5. ....

1. ....
2. ....
3. ....
4. ....
5. ....

Today's 5 things
I'm Grateful for

......./....../......

Today's 5 things
I'm Grateful for

......./....../......

1. ....
2. ....
3. ....
4. ....
5. ....

1. ....
2. ....
3. ....
4. ....
5. ....

Today's 5 things
I'm Grateful for

......./....../......

Today's 5 things
I'm Grateful for

......./....../......

1. ....
2. ....
3. ....
4. ....
5. ....

Today's 5 things
I'm Grateful for

....../...../......

1. ....
2. ....
3. ....
4. ....
5. ....

1. ....
2. ....
3. ....
4. ....
5. ....

Today's 5 things
I'm Grateful for

....../...../......

• •

My Weekly Notes

....
....
....
....
....
....
....
....
....
....

Today's 5 things
I'm Grateful for

......./....../......

1. ....
2. ....
3. ....
4. ....
5. ....

1. ....
2. ....
3. ....
4. ....
5. ....

Today's 5 things
I'm Grateful for

......./....../......

Today's 5 things
I'm Grateful for

......./....../......

1. ....
2. ....
3. ....
4. ....
5. ....

1. ....
2. ....
3. ....
4. ....
5. ....

Today's 5 things
I'm Grateful for

......./....../......

Today's 5 things
I'm Grateful for

......./....../......

1. ....
2. ....
3. ....
4. ....
5. ....

Today's 5 things
I'm Grateful for

....../....../......

1. ....
2. ....
3. ....
4. ....
5. ....

1. ....
2. ....
3. ....
4. ....
5. ....

Today's 5 things
I'm Grateful for

....../....../......

• •

My Weekly Notes

....
....
....
....
....
....
....
....
....
....

Today's 5 things
I'm Grateful for

...../...../.....

1. ....
2. ....
3. ....
4. ....
5. ....

1. ....
2. ....
3. ....
4. ....
5. ....

Today's 5 things
I'm Grateful for

...../...../.....

Today's 5 things
I'm Grateful for

...../...../.....

1. ....
2. ....
3. ....
4. ....
5. ....

1. ....
2. ....
3. ....
4. ....
5. ....

Today's 5 things
I'm Grateful for

...../...../.....

Today's 5 things
I'm Grateful for

...../...../.....

1. ....
2. ....
3. ....
4. ....
5. ....

Today's 5 things
I'm Grateful for

...../...../.....

1. ....
2. ....
3. ....
4. ....
5. ....

1. ....
2. ....
3. ....
4. ....
5. ....

Today's 5 things
I'm Grateful for

...../...../.....

• •

My Weekly Notes

....
....
....
....
....
....
....
....
....
....

Today's 5 things
I'm Grateful for

....../...../......

1. ....
2. ....
3. ....
4. ....
5. ....

1. ....
2. ....
3. ....
4. ....
5. ....

Today's 5 things
I'm Grateful for

....../...../......

Today's 5 things
I'm Grateful for

....../...../......

1. ....
2. ....
3. ....
4. ....
5. ....

1. ....
2. ....
3. ....
4. ....
5. ....

Today's 5 things
I'm Grateful for

....../...../......

Today's 5 things
I'm Grateful for

....../...../......

1. ....
2. ....
3. ....
4. ....
5. ....

Today's 5 things
I'm Grateful for

....../...../......

1. ....
2. ....
3. ....
4. ....
5. ....

1. ....
2. ....
3. ....
4. ....
5. ....

Today's 5 things
I'm Grateful for

....../...../......

• •

My Weekly Notes

....
....
....
....
....
....
....
....
....
....

Today's 5 things
I'm Grateful for

..... / ..... / .....

1. ....
2. ....
3. ....
4. ....
5. ....

1. ....
2. ....
3. ....
4. ....
5. ....

Today's 5 things
I'm Grateful for

..... / ..... / .....

Today's 5 things
I'm Grateful for

..... / ..... / .....

1. ....
2. ....
3. ....
4. ....
5. ....

1. ....
2. ....
3. ....
4. ....
5. ....

Today's 5 things
I'm Grateful for

..... / ..... / .....

Today's 5 things
I'm Grateful for

..... / ..... / .....

1. ....
2. ....
3. ....
4. ....
5. ....

Today's 5 things
I'm Grateful for

...../...../......

1. ....
2. ....
3. ....
4. ....
5. ....

1. ....
2. ....
3. ....
4. ....
5. ....

Today's 5 things
I'm Grateful for

...../...../......

My Weekly Notes

....
....
....
....
....
....
....
....
....
....

Today's 5 things
I'm Grateful for

...../...../.....

1. ....
2. ....
3. ....
4. ....
5. ....

1. ....
2. ....
3. ....
4. ....
5. ....

Today's 5 things
I'm Grateful for

...../...../.....

Today's 5 things
I'm Grateful for

...../...../.....

1. ....
2. ....
3. ....
4. ....
5. ....

1. ....
2. ....
3. ....
4. ....
5. ....

Today's 5 things
I'm Grateful for

...../...../.....

Today's 5 things
I'm Grateful for

...../...../.....

1. ....
2. ....
3. ....
4. ....
5. ....

Today's 5 things
I'm Grateful for

......./...../.....

1. ....
2. ....
3. ....
4. ....
5. ....

1. ....
2. ....
3. ....
4. ....
5. ....

Today's 5 things
I'm Grateful for

......./...../.....

My Weekly Notes

....
....
....
....
....
....
....
....
....
....

Today's 5 things
I'm Grateful for

......./....../......

1. ....
2. ....
3. ....
4. ....
5. ....

1. ....
2. ....
3. ....
4. ....
5. ....

Today's 5 things
I'm Grateful for

......./....../......

Today's 5 things
I'm Grateful for

......./....../......

1. ....
2. ....
3. ....
4. ....
5. ....

1. ....
2. ....
3. ....
4. ....
5. ....

Today's 5 things
I'm Grateful for

......./....../......

Today's 5 things
I'm Grateful for

......./....../......

1. ....
2. ....
3. ....
4. ....
5. ....

Today's 5 things
I'm Grateful for

...../...../......

1...
2...
3...
4...
5...

1...
2...
3...
4...
5...

Today's 5 things
I'm Grateful for

...../...../......

My Weekly Notes

....
....
....
....
....
....
....
....
....
....

Today's 5 things
I'm Grateful for

...../...../......

1. ....
2. ....
3. ....
4. ....
5. ....

1. ....
2. ....
3. ....
4. ....
5. ....

Today's 5 things
I'm Grateful for

...../...../......

Today's 5 things
I'm Grateful for

...../...../......

1. ....
2. ....
3. ....
4. ....
5. ....

1. ....
2. ....
3. ....
4. ....
5. ....

Today's 5 things
I'm Grateful for

...../...../......

Today's 5 things
I'm Grateful for

...../...../......

1. ....
2. ....
3. ....
4. ....
5. ....

Today's 5 things
I'm Grateful for

...../...../.....

1. ....
2. ....
3. ....
4. ....
5. ....

1. ....
2. ....
3. ....
4. ....
5. ....

Today's 5 things
I'm Grateful for

...../...../.....

• •

My Weekly Notes

....
....
....
....
....
....
....
....
....
....

Today's 5 things
I'm Grateful for

...../...../.....

1. ....
2. ....
3. ....
4. ....
5. ....

1. ....
2. ....
3. ....
4. ....
5. ....

Today's 5 things
I'm Grateful for

...../...../.....

Today's 5 things
I'm Grateful for

...../...../.....

1. ....
2. ....
3. ....
4. ....
5. ....

1. ....
2. ....
3. ....
4. ....
5. ....

Today's 5 things
I'm Grateful for

...../...../.....

Today's 5 things
I'm Grateful for

...../...../.....

1. ....
2. ....
3. ....
4. ....
5. ....

Today's 5 things
I'm Grateful for

.....*/*....*/*.....

1. ....
2. ....
3. ....
4. ....
5. ....

1. ....
2. ....
3. ....
4. ....
5. ....

Today's 5 things
I'm Grateful for

.....*/*....*/*.....

• •

My Weekly Notes

....
....
....
....
....
....
....
....
....
....

Today's 5 things
I'm Grateful for

...../...../......

1. ....
2. ....
3. ....
4. ....
5. ....

1. ....
2. ....
3. ....
4. ....
5. ....

Today's 5 things
I'm Grateful for

...../...../......

Today's 5 things
I'm Grateful for

...../...../......

1. ....
2. ....
3. ....
4. ....
5. ....

1. ....
2. ....
3. ....
4. ....
5. ....

Today's 5 things
I'm Grateful for

...../...../......

Today's 5 things
I'm Grateful for

...../...../......

1. ....
2. ....
3. ....
4. ....
5. ....

Today's 5 things
I'm Grateful for

....../....../......

1. ....
2. ....
3. ....
4. ....
5. ....

1. ....
2. ....
3. ....
4. ....
5. ....

Today's 5 things
I'm Grateful for

....../....../......

• •

My Weekly Notes

....
....
....
....
....
....
....
....
....
....

Today's 5 things
I'm Grateful for

......./....../......

1. ....
2. ....
3. ....
4. ....
5. ....

1. ....
2. ....
3. ....
4. ....
5. ....

Today's 5 things
I'm Grateful for

......./....../......

Today's 5 things
I'm Grateful for

......./....../......

1. ....
2. ....
3. ....
4. ....
5. ....

1. ....
2. ....
3. ....
4. ....
5. ....

Today's 5 things
I'm Grateful for

......./....../......

Today's 5 things
I'm Grateful for

......./....../......

1. ....
2. ....
3. ....
4. ....
5. ....

Today's 5 things
I'm Grateful for

....../...../......

1...
2...
3...
4...
5...

1...
2...
3...
4...
5...

Today's 5 things
I'm Grateful for

....../...../......

My Weekly Notes

....
....
....
....
....
....
....
....
....
....

Today's 5 things
I'm Grateful for

....../...../......

1. ....
2. ....
3. ....
4. ....
5. ....

1. ....
2. ....
3. ....
4. ....
5. ....

Today's 5 things
I'm Grateful for

....../...../......

Today's 5 things
I'm Grateful for

....../...../......

1. ....
2. ....
3. ....
4. ....
5. ....

1. ....
2. ....
3. ....
4. ....
5. ....

Today's 5 things
I'm Grateful for

....../...../......

Today's 5 things
I'm Grateful for

....../...../......

1. ....
2. ....
3. ....
4. ....
5. ....

Today's 5 things
I'm Grateful for

....../...../......

1. ....
2. ....
3. ....
4. ....
5. ....

1. ....
2. ....
3. ....
4. ....
5. ....

Today's 5 things
I'm Grateful for

....../...../......

• •

My Weekly Notes

....
....
....
....
....
....
....
....
....

Today's 5 things
I'm Grateful for

......./......./.......

1. ....
2. ....
3. ....
4. ....
5. ....

1. ....
2. ....
3. ....
4. ....
5. ....

Today's 5 things
I'm Grateful for

......./......./.......

Today's 5 things
I'm Grateful for

......./......./.......

1. ....
2. ....
3. ....
4. ....
5. ....

1. ....
2. ....
3. ....
4. ....
5. ....

Today's 5 things
I'm Grateful for

......./......./.......

Today's 5 things
I'm Grateful for

......./......./.......

1. ....
2. ....
3. ....
4. ....
5. ....

Today's 5 things
I'm Grateful for

...../...../......

1. ....
2. ....
3. ....
4. ....
5. ....

1. ....
2. ....
3. ....
4. ....
5. ....

Today's 5 things
I'm Grateful for

...../...../......

My Weekly Notes

....
....
....
....
....
....
....
....
....

Today's 5 things
I'm Grateful for

...../...../......

1. ....
2. ....
3. ....
4. ....
5. ....

1. ....
2. ....
3. ....
4. ....
5. ....

Today's 5 things
I'm Grateful for

...../...../......

Today's 5 things
I'm Grateful for

...../...../......

1. ....
2. ....
3. ....
4. ....
5. ....

1. ....
2. ....
3. ....
4. ....
5. ....

Today's 5 things
I'm Grateful for

...../...../......

Today's 5 things
I'm Grateful for

...../...../......

1. ....
2. ....
3. ....
4. ....
5. ....

Today's 5 things
I'm Grateful for

......./....../......

1. ....
2. ....
3. ....
4. ....
5. ....

1. ....
2. ....
3. ....
4. ....
5. ....

Today's 5 things
I'm Grateful for

......./....../......

My Weekly Notes

....
....
....
....
....
....
....
....
....
....

Today's 5 things
I'm Grateful for

...... / ..... / ......

1. ....
2. ....
3. ....
4. ....
5. ....

1. ....
2. ....
3. ....
4. ....
5. ....

Today's 5 things
I'm Grateful for

...... / ..... / ......

Today's 5 things
I'm Grateful for

...... / ..... / ......

1. ....
2. ....
3. ....
4. ....
5. ....

1. ....
2. ....
3. ....
4. ....
5. ....

Today's 5 things
I'm Grateful for

...... / ..... / ......

Today's 5 things
I'm Grateful for

...... / ..... / ......

1. ....
2. ....
3. ....
4. ....
5. ....

Today's 5 things
I'm Grateful for

......./....../......

1. ....
2. ....
3. ....
4. ....
5. ....

1. ....
2. ....
3. ....
4. ....
5. ....

Today's 5 things
I'm Grateful for

......./....../......

• •

My Weekly Notes

....
....
....
....
....
....
....
....
....
....

Today's 5 things
I'm Grateful for

...../...../......

1. ....
2. ....
3. ....
4. ....
5. ....

1. ....
2. ....
3. ....
4. ....
5. ....

Today's 5 things
I'm Grateful for

...../...../......

Today's 5 things
I'm Grateful for

...../...../......

1. ....
2. ....
3. ....
4. ....
5. ....

1. ....
2. ....
3. ....
4. ....
5. ....

Today's 5 things
I'm Grateful for

...../...../......

Today's 5 things
I'm Grateful for

...../...../......

1. ....
2. ....
3. ....
4. ....
5. ....

Today's 5 things
I'm Grateful for

......./......./......

1. ....
2. ....
3. ....
4. ....
5. ....

1. ....
2. ....
3. ....
4. ....
5. ....

Today's 5 things
I'm Grateful for

......./......./......

• •

My Weekly Notes

....
....
....
....
....
....
....
....
....
....

Today's 5 things
I'm Grateful for

......./......./.......

1. ....
2. ....
3. ....
4. ....
5. ....

1. ....
2. ....
3. ....
4. ....
5. ....

Today's 5 things
I'm Grateful for

......./......./.......

Today's 5 things
I'm Grateful for

......./......./.......

1. ....
2. ....
3. ....
4. ....
5. ....

1. ....
2. ....
3. ....
4. ....
5. ....

Today's 5 things
I'm Grateful for

......./......./.......

Today's 5 things
I'm Grateful for

......./......./.......

1. ....
2. ....
3. ....
4. ....
5. ....

Today's 5 things
I'm Grateful for

.....*/*.....*/*.....

1. ....
2. ....
3. ....
4. ....
5. ....

1. ....
2. ....
3. ....
4. ....
5. ....

Today's 5 things
I'm Grateful for

.....*/*.....*/*.....

• •

My Weekly Notes

....
....
....
....
....
....
....
....
....
....

Today's 5 things
I'm Grateful for

...../...../.....

1. ....
2. ....
3. ....
4. ....
5. ....

1. ....
2. ....
3. ....
4. ....
5. ....

Today's 5 things
I'm Grateful for

...../...../.....

Today's 5 things
I'm Grateful for

...../...../.....

1. ....
2. ....
3. ....
4. ....
5. ....

1. ....
2. ....
3. ....
4. ....
5. ....

Today's 5 things
I'm Grateful for

...../...../.....

Today's 5 things
I'm Grateful for

...../...../.....

1. ....
2. ....
3. ....
4. ....
5. ....

Today's 5 things
I'm Grateful for

....../...../.....

1. ....
2. ....
3. ....
4. ....
5. ....

1. ....
2. ....
3. ....
4. ....
5. ....

Today's 5 things
I'm Grateful for

....../...../.....

• •

My Weekly Notes

....
....
....
....
....
....
....
....
....
....

Today's 5 things
I'm Grateful for

......./....../......

1. ....
2. ....
3. ....
4. ....
5. ....

1. ....
2. ....
3. ....
4. ....
5. ....

Today's 5 things
I'm Grateful for

......./....../......

Today's 5 things
I'm Grateful for

......./....../......

1. ....
2. ....
3. ....
4. ....
5. ....

1. ....
2. ....
3. ....
4. ....
5. ....

Today's 5 things
I'm Grateful for

......./....../......

Today's 5 things
I'm Grateful for

......./....../......

1. ....
2. ....
3. ....
4. ....
5. ....

Today's 5 things
I'm Grateful for

...../...../......

1...
2...
3...
4...
5...

1...
2...
3...
4...
5...

Today's 5 things
I'm Grateful for

...../...../......

• •

My Weekly Notes

....
....
....
....
....
....
....
....
....
....

Today's 5 things
I'm Grateful for

....../...../......

1. ....
2. ....
3. ....
4. ....
5. ....

1. ....
2. ....
3. ....
4. ....
5. ....

Today's 5 things
I'm Grateful for

....../...../......

Today's 5 things
I'm Grateful for

....../...../......

1. ....
2. ....
3. ....
4. ....
5. ....

1. ....
2. ....
3. ....
4. ....
5. ....

Today's 5 things
I'm Grateful for

....../...../......

Today's 5 things
I'm Grateful for

....../...../......

1. ....
2. ....
3. ....
4. ....
5. ....

Today's 5 things
I'm Grateful for

...../...../......

1. ....
2. ....
3. ....
4. ....
5. ....

1. ....
2. ....
3. ....
4. ....
5. ....

Today's 5 things
I'm Grateful for

...../...../......

• •

My Weekly Notes

....
....
....
....
....
....
....
....
....
....

Today's 5 things
I'm Grateful for

...../...../......

1. ....
2. ....
3. ....
4. ....
5. ....

1. ....
2. ....
3. ....
4. ....
5. ....

Today's 5 things
I'm Grateful for

...../...../......

Today's 5 things
I'm Grateful for

...../...../......

1. ....
2. ....
3. ....
4. ....
5. ....

1. ....
2. ....
3. ....
4. ....
5. ....

Today's 5 things
I'm Grateful for

...../...../......

Today's 5 things
I'm Grateful for

...../...../......

1. ....
2. ....
3. ....
4. ....
5. ....

Today's 5 things
I'm Grateful for

......./......./.......

1. ....
2. ....
3. ....
4. ....
5. ....

1. ....
2. ....
3. ....
4. ....
5. ....

Today's 5 things
I'm Grateful for

......./......./.......

• • • • • • • ● ● ● ● ● ● ● ● ● ● • • • • • •

My Weekly Notes

....
....
....
....
....
....
....
....
....

Today's 5 things
I'm Grateful for

...../...../......

1. ....
2. ....
3. ....
4. ....
5. ....

1. ....
2. ....
3. ....
4. ....
5. ....

Today's 5 things
I'm Grateful for

...../...../......

Today's 5 things
I'm Grateful for

...../...../......

1. ....
2. ....
3. ....
4. ....
5. ....

1. ....
2. ....
3. ....
4. ....
5. ....

Today's 5 things
I'm Grateful for

...../...../......

Today's 5 things
I'm Grateful for

...../...../......

1. ....
2. ....
3. ....
4. ....
5. ....

Today's 5 things
I'm Grateful for

....../....../......

1. ....
2. ....
3. ....
4. ....
5. ....

1. ....
2. ....
3. ....
4. ....
5. ....

Today's 5 things
I'm Grateful for

....../....../......

• •

My Weekly Notes

....
....
....
....
....
....
....
....
....
....

Today's 5 things
I'm Grateful for

......./....../......

1. ....
2. ....
3. ....
4. ....
5. ....

1. ....
2. ....
3. ....
4. ....
5. ....

Today's 5 things
I'm Grateful for

......./....../......

Today's 5 things
I'm Grateful for

......./....../......

1. ....
2. ....
3. ....
4. ....
5. ....

1. ....
2. ....
3. ....
4. ....
5. ....

Today's 5 things
I'm Grateful for

......./....../......

Today's 5 things
I'm Grateful for

......./....../......

1. ....
2. ....
3. ....
4. ....
5. ....

Today's 5 things
I'm Grateful for

....../...../......

1. ....
2. ....
3. ....
4. ....
5. ....

1. ....
2. ....
3. ....
4. ....
5. ....

Today's 5 things
I'm Grateful for

....../...../......

My Weekly Notes

....
....
....
....
....
....
....
....
....
....

Today's 5 things

I'm Grateful for

....../...../......

1. ....
2. ....
3. ....
4. ....
5. ....

1. ....
2. ....
3. ....
4. ....
5. ....

Today's 5 things

I'm Grateful for

....../...../......

Today's 5 things

I'm Grateful for

....../...../......

1. ....
2. ....
3. ....
4. ....
5. ....

1. ....
2. ....
3. ....
4. ....
5. ....

Today's 5 things

I'm Grateful for

....../...../......

Today's 5 things

I'm Grateful for

....../...../......

1. ....
2. ....
3. ....
4. ....
5. ....

Today's 5 things
I'm Grateful for

......./....../......

1. ....
2. ....
3. ....
4. ....
5. ....

1. ....
2. ....
3. ....
4. ....
5. ....

Today's 5 things
I'm Grateful for

......./....../......

• •

My Weekly Notes

....
....
....
....
....
....
....
....
....
....

Made in the USA
Monee, IL
12 December 2020